LITTLE HUMAN RELICS

Poems

Amanda Williams

I am grateful to the following journals for including some of these poems in their pages: *Cactus Heart Magazine* (Catalysis), *Artemis: A Journal for Artists and Writers from the Blue Ridge Region* (Earl), *The Red Truck Review* (Bedtime Story), *Jam Tarts Magazine* (In Orbit), *Sugar House Review* (On Rural Marriage), *Silver Birch Press* (Letter to Santa), and *The Academy of American Poets/Poets.org* (What I Need From You).

For my family, und für Emerenz

Contents

Morning, 13th Street, Roanoke, VA   1

Self Portraits in Tempera   2

Earl   3

I baked a cake yesterday afternoon   4

I Will Perform the Rite Until   5

Pasture Requiem   6

On Rural Marriage   8

Culpa   9

The Art of Alterations   11

Love, In Season   12

The Decoy   14

Bedtime Story   16

Letter to Santa   18

In Orbit   20

Catalysis   21

Beauty Hacks   22

An Alhambrian Idyll   23

What I Need from You   24

Heartsick   26

Of This, I Am Certain   28

Brotzeit   29

Morning, 13th Street, Roanoke, VA

A cardinal sits like a blood drop in the brume, and I think
of the old country, mist woven into the nests of sugar beet fields,
the mountains of harvest piled up along the paths, stark-white

muddled with brown, a pile of unearthed skulls. From the high point
of the hill behind my family's sprawling farm, the twin spires
of Haindling jut up from the village with quiet confidence;

they have been here for four-hundred years. They know
they will outlive you—straight, ivory fingers which God holds up
to his lips to hush us as we twist and fret about eternity.

From this elevation, I can see a huddle of smooth, amber-colored cows
standing with their backs to one another, tails hanging like flags
on a windless battlement, snouts leaning into the blank slate of fog.

They are waiting for the wolf, they are waiting for the farmer.
They stubbornly stand their ground thick-headed with imagined bravery,
though there can be no real defense. God must be in them,

and this their prayer-circle; he wishes us to be faithful in the face
of danger, not to ripple our hides at the stinging fly, lest we turn
and find the real danger already at our throats. The cardinal shivers

the rain from his back, and who knows if he trembles with fear
or delight; he will fly away soon, and I will still be here, skull piled up
with strange thoughts, white finger helpless to silence them.

Self Portraits in Tempera

-after wall paintings in the old Recreation Room, St. Albans Sanatorium, Radford, Virginia

They drove you mad with shocks,
drowned your wails in water, garnished
all you ate with lithium, and still
you had the foresight to leave us
these runes, these hieroglyphs
daubed on the now-peeling plaster
of the old Recreation Room.

Your portrait of a woman
is a cave-drawing, a blue triangle
with a thumbprint head floating
above that geometric body,
such sharp edges, the thin lines
of its arms outstretched.

You were given more colors
for good behavior, you painted
a blue and yellow bird you once saw
from the window of the Rocking Room.
They strapped you into a lolling chair
and you sucked in every line and shadow
of that bird, the way her wings
flattened to her sides as she dove
through the air, and you've painted her here

just so. She is diving, face-first
toward the tile floor with a blood-
spattered bandage (you were so good,
they gave you red paint too) bound
around her wings. She cannot fly.
She is on the way to her treatment,
left here to remind us how.

Earl

The temperature of the rain falls
as the heart does, without warning.
The thicket of thought is dark already,
my clumps of memory yawn
to admit you after this long year
of oblivion. All those wretched nights
spent soused in self-medication collapse
as your voice comes through the open window
as if from another life. The bass, Germanic growl,
the oily vowels working into my brain
like a busy worm, rotting the core
into a fragile pulp that is so much more capable
of love.

My Erl King, luring young girls to your bed
where love is made and unmade again,
the hearth not warm enough to keep
our bodies from cooling after you skin us
down to our lusty, rust-red sinews.

I am on that dark path again; I follow
the fox and the hare to your low doorway,
your body bristling and fresh against the rotting
timber frame. Beyond the door is the smoldering hearth
where I will lay on a bear skin and be lovingly stripped
beneath the hanging bundles of herbs
and strung-up doves.

How glad I was to stop seeing you
in the trees. I can't go back to the horror
of the whole forest staring.

I baked a cake yesterday afternoon

I baked a cake yesterday afternoon,
and it didn't turn out. From this, I knew
our love was ruined. Something about
the consistency was wrong, the cake
had collapsed in the center, capsizing
inward from the edges, which had burned.
I used an organic flour substitute,
flax-seed meal, and the texture of the batter
was thick and gritty, grating the roof
of my mouth like your passive, rude muttering
minced my heart to shreds. I should
have known not to bother baking it,
but I did what I always do—wrap
all my hopes around a thing, tightly
as a tourniquet, and thrust it toward the heat
to see what scorches, what is left to forge.

I Will Perform the Rite Until

-after Emerenz Meier's "Johannisfeuer"

I coil my legs and jump, clear the edge of the bed
and land in the burning valley of your stomach,
one knee on each side of your oil-drum chest, the wiry hairs
snapping like dry twigs, my own belly-skin pinking
from the iridescent heat. You are the pyre, the effigy

that I have labored to build, I have gathered all manner of wood
together and lashed it with tight threads from my heart.
The neighbors watched round-eyed as I drug table legs
and whiskey crates up the front stairs, through the door.
I littered the yard with giant cable spools
for your eyes, bundles of ash twigs from the park.

I build you so I can burn you every night, strike my arm
like a match against your sweat-slick skin and watch
as you blaze up, my king, my wicker-man. Your roaring face
fanned by my undulations, more breath, more sweat dropping, sizzling
in midair like a sprinkling of gasoline, faster, cries curl
from my mouth like smoke, and I say *this is the ancient rite—*

take my hand and jump. And you do, and something
inside of me leaps with you, leaps, flickers, and goes out.
Year after year, millions perform themselves to cinders,
lay in the cooling after-ash and murmur *this love
will work.* What else are we to do but gather those ashes,
pray for daughters, and scatter them in our gardens?

Pasture Requiem

New horses in your pasture. The first day,
they cantered up from the creek-bottom
to greet me as you once did, but with the cordiality
of strangers, their probing noses marking me
as *other*. Now, they encircle, fold me into the herd
of two, now three, me sans-tail and we look
like a 10-legged monster, huddling. They guard
against dangers they've sensed in the two weeks
since they arrived: The neighbor's dogs who slip
into the dark barn, my father who fires rounds

into the pond, killing snappers. They must
have heard the coyotes the very first night,
bold and desperate with the falling temperatures,
loping all the way up to the barn, ricocheting
their howls against the frozen tin. We linger
on your grave, the knoll of dirt and lime
perpetually sinking as the earth swaddles
your sweet bones. If they knew—would they be afraid?
Would their eye-whites express the fear
that only horse-eyes can, orbs rolling like marbles

cast from a cup, nostrils flared and scarlet
with the effort of heaving those huge lungs,
each as big as a sack of seed corn?
Nothing trembles now in the grey
but four ears, pricking, swiveling
like petal-soft radars toward a winter bird
rustling in a nest. They tuck their muzzles,
wreathed in smoke, against my abdomen.
I fear a cinder of joy leaping up from my heart's
cellar, kindled by their hay-and-wild-onion smell,
their grain-and-sticky-molasses breath—

they are not you, and they do not know
how I held you in this very spot, sprawled on the grass
like when you first fell from your mother,
twenty-two years before I gave you to the ground.
They have eaten the clover that grows
on your burial mound, they have rolled
themselves into capes of dark mud, as you did,
set their crescent hooves in your old tracks,
which rain, moss, and weeds had near filled in—

how can they not know? I heave the rust-hinged
pasture gate closed and lock the clinking chain.
Through the spectral fog I am touched
by the quiet probes of their dark eyes
that follow me back to the house.

Go on, get. Run with them.

On Rural Marriage

On my parents' anniversary, my mother circled
the glass cases of the gun counter at Walmart,
asked which bullets flew the fastest
from the barrel, which would shatter
bone. She selected a box of Remington 12-gauge shells
and a gun-cleaning kit, and she wrapped them up
with a card that said, "I still love you." She lay
half-awake that night, wondering when he would join her,
fill the empty half of the bed, now as cold
as a steel muzzle before a shot. She turned,
and through the cracked bedroom door saw him
in the dimly lit kitchen, slowly polishing the stock.

Culpa

As a child, my eye was trained to follow the line of blood
        loping down
over the lacquered chest of Jesus. I sat on rough pine pews, a draft

from the clerestory swirling down, smoothing the flagstones,
        gently lifting
a lock of human hair from the carved forehead of the Savior

who gazed down, knowingly. The priest's words gave meaning
        to the blood,
gave praise to the hardened globules of paint, sometimes thickly daubed

about the immaculate wounds, sometimes scrolled down
        his pierced foot,
his body a manuscript illuminated with the lessons of sacrifice.

When night fell over the chattering stained glass the shadows of anguish
        grew long
on Mary's porcelain face, the strains of childbirth appeared in the waning

of her cheeks, her gold-leaf crown winked in the failing light
        and went out.
I never lingered after mass—I imagined warmth returning to that blood,

the arrows bobbing with breath in the wounded body of St. Sebastian,
        St. Michael slowly plunging
his sword into the demon's reeling chest, and all the bravery, death,

and godliness throbbing around me, noctambulous. Still, I cannot
        look away
from the gore of idols. I have no ruined flesh—if I turn my back

they will whisper among themselves that I know nothing of penance,
        that there is part of me
which I do not, and cannot know how to give to God.

The Art of Alterations

"Du Wirst Krank!"
— Singer Oma

She was up to something helpful when she snuck
into the room where her granddaughters slept
and took their summer nightgowns, pink and white
from beneath the cool pillows, sat down at her kitchen table
and snipped the ruffles from the bottom hems, plucked out
all the clinging threads, and re-fashioned them, rolled
the fabric into pleats with her bent thumbs pinning
and stitched on little sleeves to the thin spaghetti straps.

She pressed and folded the dreamy little garments
and quickly tucked them back beneath the sheets,
all before the girls returned from their play, before
they learned that there are few people in life willing
to wrap your shoulders in such honest work.

Love, In Season

Would you get down
on all fours and act
a stag for me?
Nothing could show
your form more noble,
no crown could fit
your head so well
as that imagined thorny diadem,
circlet of bone, prized
because no man
can grow his own.

Will you trot, will you throw
your snorts about and ripple
your hide for me? This is no
game; I need to see you
in a form more true
than your up-right-brained self
can perform, I need to see
you tramp the dirt with purpose
unspoken: you must give yourself
over to wildness. For this
is the only thing I trust,
your eyes glassy with the stillness
of listening, so that if a small
murmur, a leaf, dropped
from my lips, your ear
would swivel to it.

I will count your triumphs
by the spires of your antler,
I want to see your valiance
thick as a hind leg leaping.
Crown yourself with pale hooks,

12

the verdant kindnesses
of uncomplicated love, in these
lush gestures stand unfailingly,
on all fours, and know yourself—
a prize in any season.

The Decoy

Each year we place a painted owl
above our dark-stained door
to keep the songbirds from weaving
their nests into our festive pine boughs.

We wire its stiff talons to the siding
so that it looms at forty-five degrees;
a strange appendage, it looks insane,
a trail of melted snow frozen in a stripe

down its hard-feathered back.
The lacquered eyes have faded
from the stripping winds, no longer
yolk-yellow but more like the moon,

pale, still, but less beam-like.
Perhaps that is why the little sparrows
and thick-chested robins are not afraid
of it. Their wingtips brush its lifeless beak

as they bring another husk,
another sweetgum twig to weave
into the plastic needles of the bough.
The nesting birds litter our stoop

with their droppings, which despite
the frozen air do not freeze, and stain
our church shoes as we hustle to the car
while the blank-eyed owl does nothing

but twist against the eaves of the porch.
Once in the car, after a few miles,
I try to tell him how deeply I was hurt
by his words, and hear him confess

how little he knows me, but my father's silence
takes wing in the cave of leather interior
and rushes right over my head, takes no notice
of my white fingers, wired to the seat.

Bedtime Story

My ten-year-old father
furiously paddled the pirogue
across the pond
        as water crept in
through a hole.

Across the bank,
the massive bull
                bellowed, shook
        his mammoth head,
hot saliva flying,
wielding his horns
like two broadswords.

The bull paced the bank,
following
                the terrified boy
as he raced
to the other side to drag
the boat ashore
                and dump
the mutinous water.

The minute he emptied it,
the beast came charging
toward him,
                eyes raw and rolling
and my father
threw the boat back
into the bayou water
                        paddled away
as the horns grazed
the rough wooden side.

His salvation came
hours later. His grandfather,
                    fearless,
waved his battered fedora,
and the creature fled.

My father turned
to walk the long way
        back to the house
as the little boat
was finally overcome
with water,
            and sank.

Letter to Santa

"The Krampus shambles through the streets, frightening children and threatening folk with bundles of birch branches or whips made of horse tails…he often slaps the bellies of young girls with his birch club, a tradition which undoubtedly originated with pagan fertility rights."
- German Life Magazine, December 2014

Santa, where is your ugly other,
where is the one who rattled birches
against our windowpane in the shadows
of the frozen pines? I'd put my shoe
on the doorstep each December 5th,
letting out just a wisp of oven-warmed air
as I reached a small arm over the threshold
into the night to place the vessel
of judgment. By morning I'd know
what kind of child I'd been.

Santa, you have the benevolence
of God, the joviality of drunken uncles,
the plumpness of holiday roasts, and you
have never thrown a bad kid
into your red velvet sack. In fact,
when we moved to America I craved
the verdict of that goat-demon
as he prowled our second-grade classroom,
presenting poisonous gems of coal
to those who deserved no better—
and people wonder why I am so hung up
on right and wrong, accountability,
that old vigilante justice.

Santa, you've made me soft and fat
with the buttermilk of forgiveness,
with 10th place trophies, with a stocking-stuffer

for each time I cursed in front of Oma.
Fear gives gorgeous results, a child
who grasps consequence. How could we be
anything but good when the grown-ups'
jolly whispers crackled in our ears:

He will find you. He is coming.

In Orbit

-after Pindar

Again she turns her thoughts to a marriage
that was a prize open to all—why would any woman
want better than him, perfect lines of bone
and skin like untroubled water, not even a thread

of anger in a brow that never tangles. Motivation
in spades, working overtime at the office
or turning up the garden's earth, an expert planter
both of lettuces and the raw matter of children.

A prize open to all—any woman could have tilted
for him, claimed him with a running start, or crept
slowly into the corners of his dazzle-eyes; a prize
certainly for her, whose luck is always absent;

as a child, she was always short a trophy.
As a woman, she is short on money, gas,
but she is full of him. Again she turns her thoughts
to a marriage which her mother wholly endorses,

thinking that this is her big chance to hear
the tinkling and thunder of grandchildren.
A marriage—like a spoil of some war
for which young people are constantly called

to take up their beaten arms. Like an illuminated sign
over the door of your modest home, which tells
all who enter that you have not failed, you send
your own cards at Christmas, you have learned to cook,

to mend, to rise, to reckon. You are not alone.
Again she turns her thoughts—again, she turns.

Catalysis, n.

1.†Dissolution, destruction, ruin. *Obs. Rare.* i.e., The sad catalysis did come, and swept away eleven hundred thousand of the nation, and all that they had sown and bred did founder—it occurred quietly, when a mound of stale salt field-earth, laced with the tang of a horse buried last October deflated (he must have sighed, and let his tired plow-breaths out). It occurred when, just beyond the far side of the barn, perched on the farm's peak, the rains carried his essence down in rivulets, down over hoof-paths, through the thatched roots of wheat, down to the hollow, the deep womb of the pasture where, before they were drowned, pale shoots turned their faces toward the sun.

Beauty Hacks

*"Will someone please help me write my damn wedding vows? I mean, what am I supposed
to say? Happy happy joy joy, down in my heart, let's just get married and get this over
with already?'"*
                                        -overheard at the Star Nails salon

Topless and Barefoot: The lady at the counter
told me it's a good color for spring. For me,
year round. Now I wish I'd chosen *Bride-ways Glances*
or *Starter Wife*—something acrylic starts nipping away
at my heart, like my cuticles being plucked from my nail bed
one flake at a time. I could claw her eyes out
with my still-naked talons, she speaks of vows

as if they were McDoubles, and yet—I'm ashamed
to admit that I wish to step into her fake-tanned
leather jacket of a body just to have the problem
of sorting out things like rings, the list of important dates
she pops off with each smack of gum: dress-fitting,
hair appointment, cake-tasting. The jewel-encrusted lady

on my left has been eaves-dropping, says *Someone's
in for a busy few months!* The color she's having
shellacked on is called *Teal the Cows Come Home.*
I hate it. They ask me if I'm married. I should lie
or risk being dismissed from the club, they don't notice
that the little tray on my station, which exists only to hold
the customer's rings while her hands are dipped, scrubbed,

filed, and clipped, is empty. My nail tech has probed
underneath my nail too forcefully, and then drowns
my finger in acetone. *So, you have big plans tonight?
You gotta date?* The "bride" has chosen her color,
Tart With a Heart. Something stings. *You gotta boyfriend?*
My empty finger is tipped with a big red sign.
Don't worry, honey, someone out there's gonna love you.

An Alhambrian Idyll

"...in the fields the heifer
Looks up at the sky and sniffs the change in the air
With open nostrils..."
                                     -Virgil, the First Georgic

Once the air turns humid, their heads begin to drift
downward. They cave in to the ground,
thick knee joints collapsing beneath them
until they are folded up under their vast bellies.
There they lay, chewing, the cow-mystics.
The farmers abide by these dusty, four-legged oracles.
When they see them settling on the ground
they park their tractors, close up their barns,
their wives collect the laundry from the line.
The sky grows black over Bond County,
menacing, as the first drops of rain are shed
from the gathering clouds. The terrific storm comes,
and the lightning passes over the land, striking nothing.

What I Need from You

Let the longing slip
down the throat,
tipped down into
that poisoned well.
Titillate, let the tuft
and trail run over
the mouth, under.

We rear, and someone
is ragged at the door,
lisping the dust
from beneath the slot,
the frame, the dirt, hark.

Kick and tickle,
that I might be warmed
and the seed may take,
dandle, dawdle, dip it
from my pool of secrets,
metal ladle, lick the rust.

Can this be
the right address,
this ticking old fence,
this leaning rocker,
this dark and dismal?
Declare that I am of it,
and I'll go in.

Acutiator, will you whet
my lips on your stone
when I am dulled,
when the battlefield's
gone cold? Accept this,

24

your office, trumpet,
hack, sharpen.

Protect me, hound,
helper, hand-holder;
the disease of virgins
creeps in the blood,
and the bunting is hung.
I am riddled with field-rows,
plowed by your fingers—
promise, pluck.

Heartsick

-after Emerenz Meier's "Trübe Stimmung"

Had I only chosen the woods.
Song and spruce, lost things
sleeping in tree whorls,
villages of moss, proud

little birds. Good kind
of shade, not that tar-black
that eats the finish
from bumpers, that cakes thick

in shoe treads. I fling
a lament at the nearest
shrub, weed—growing things
understand me well, they pray

right back. I've chirped
till I'm tired, till
I've mingled with every last
body, and all the lit-up

screens beeping in pain.
Had I only chosen the woods.
The gentler sounds
try and slip into my ears,

which have grown thick
as dumbbells. There's nothing
left for me in the villages.
My skin dreams of the creek,

a silver grave: my foot
has abandoned the road.

I cannot wait until I am dead
for such peace—I go.

Of This, I Am Certain

If we have not died before the end of this year,
we will walk amid the bright mantle of autumn.
We will wake during the elongating nights, realize
that we have wandered apart in sleep, and once again
drape ourselves around one another like a sweater
over a chair back. We will bite the whitening air
as it wisps from our mouths, twirling our speech
toward the sun. We will witness children readying
their hearts for snow, and all that is to come.

And if we have not died before the end of this month,
we will celebrate the day we met with wine
and volleys of memory, casks of well-aged love hoisted up
from their resting place. We will take that trip out of town,
we will pack all of our little human relics into your car
and take the road thick with trees, the one which climbs and climbs.
We will nest ourselves wherever we land.

And if we have not died before the end of this moment,
we will plan to go to dinner on Saturday, I will call my mother
to hear about the raucous thriving of my family, you will settle
on the couch to watch the game. We will meet each other's eyes
as you pass by my half-open bedroom door, and in
that moment realize what is meant by *forever*.

Brotzeit

-for Opa

I have set our places with modest plates
upon which a thousand small fasts

have been broken. Half of a cucumber
from the shadows of the *Speisekammer*,

sliced, and laid as neat as a field row.
Tomato quartered and dusted with pepper,

a soft block of butter, uncovered. Paper-thin
pieces of salami folded and nested, the many edges

dense as blooms. Dark bread unwrapped
from a cloth, seeds scattered on the floor,

re-sown in the woodgrain. I have laid out
the rude tools we need, and with that my hands

have performed the magic of women,
to make much out of little, to care, to

conjure—See, Opa has already taken
his place, *Erl Bräu* froths as we pray.

www.ingramcontent.com/pod-product-compliance
Lightning Source LLC
Chambersburg PA
CBHW031155090426
42738CB00008B/1346